Rou

Congrats on
Promotion. And the launch of the
next chapter in your sales career!

In The Absence of Value, All That's Left is $$

Rik Van

In the Absence of Value, All That's Left is $$

THINGS YOUR FATHER NEVER TAUGHT YOU ABOUT SALES

Rik Vonderhaar

ISBN: 1548278548
ISBN 13: 9781548278540
Library of Congress Control Number: 2017909870
CreateSpace Independent Publishing Platform
North Charleston, South Carolina

CONTENTS

Introduction · vii

Element 1   Positivity · 1

Element 2   Preparation · 3

Element 3   Be Real · 7

Element 4   Warm Up (Getting to Know You) · · · · · · · · · · · · · · 11

Element 5   NEADS Analysis (Solution Selling) · · · · · · · · · · · · · 17

Element 6   Company Information · 20

Element 7   Product Information · 23

Element 8   Trial-Closes · 26

Element 9   The Investment (a.k.a. Negotiating) · · · · · · · · · · · · · 28

Element 10   Handling Objections · 39

Element 11   Paperwork · 47

Element 12 Warm Down · 50

Element 13 What's Next· 52

Final Thoughts · 57

About the Author · 59

INTRODUCTION

When I first thought about a title for this book, I contemplated using *In the Absence of Quality, All You Have Is Price.* But when I looked up the word "quality" in *Webster's Dictionary*, its definition of "that which makes something what it is" just didn't correlate with the point I wanted to make. Hence, the choice of the word "value," which is defined as "that which is desirable or worthy for its own sake; worth, or the degree of worth."

In sales, consumers often purchase higher-end products because of the perceived value in the quality of the product. This is why Mercedes-Benz dealerships are still in operation. And I guarantee you that when a Mercedes salesperson shows a vehicle, he or she focuses on the features, advantages, and benefits and not just the cost. Otherwise, their sales would be very poor. People want to know what they are getting for their money (a.k.a. value) so they can make an educated decision. The point is, in the absence of value, all that's left is price.

In this book, I will be taking you through the "elements" in making a sale. Why elements? Well, I believe that selling is elementary, something that can be learned with effort (just like you did in grade school). And remember, in science, elements combined with other elements make some of the most exciting products we use on a daily basis:

- Sodium (Na) + Chloride (Cl) = Salt
- Hydrogen (H) + Oxygen (2O) = Water
- Iron (Fe) + Manganese (Mn) = Steel
- Copper (Cu) + Zinc (Zn) = Brass

Just like a miner finding gold or silver in a mine, you will have several nuggets to "take away" with you—that will have a great deal of worth.

After your first trip through this book, you will be in a better position to understand the elements of a sale, from the perspective of either the salesperson or the consumer. You will learn about the importance of being real, the importance of body language, some tips on negotiating, as well as lots of other nuggets.

Caution: If you are looking for a book that will teach you how to close, you are missing the point. In sales, the entire process contributes to the close. It would be like asking for help to win a PGA tournament by teaching you how to putt; a professional golfer does a lot more to win a tournament than putting.

Are you ready to be a sponge and absorb as much as you can? Can you have an open mind to learn? If yes, then go to Element 1. If no, simply return this book to the shelf and keep doing what you are doing. And good luck with that, because when you keep doing the same things, expecting different results...well, you know the rest.

Before you begin: Each of the next thirteen elements are the "value blocks" you continue to build upon that will lead you to a sale. Some are clearly seen by your customers, and some are not. But when you add them up, the value blocks provide the reasons why you, your interactions with the customers, your questions, your company, your warranty, and your products, to name a few, provide your customers with the desire to say yes to your investment. It's like the game of Jenga —your goal is to build as many value blocks as possible, being careful not to cause a collapse by beginning to talk about the investment until it's time. You have to decide if you want to make your presentation all about value, using the thirteen Elements, or just about price. Forgive me if I am repeating myself, but it is vitally important that you make the right decision.

And, at the end of each Element, I ask you to write down your takeaway nugget(s) from that element. I could share with you what I believe are the most important takeaway nuggets, but I don't know you and what you want to improve upon. Obviously you wanted to learn and make some changes in your sales process, or you would not have purchased this book. So, be a good student and jot down your takeaway nuggets. More on what you should do with the nuggets you've selected at the end of the book. And, yes, it's OK to write in your book, because you own it.

ELEMENT 1

POSITIVITY

*Positive thinking will let you do everything
better than negative thinking will.*
—ZIG ZIGLAR

*Once you replace negative thoughts with positive
ones, you'll start having positive results.*
—WILLIE NELSON

Two men from very different backgrounds, yet they both feel the same about positivity!

- Always think positive—have PMA (positive mental attitude). You need to always be aware of how you are feeling. When you begin to think negative, reach into your memory vault and bring forward a good thought or a good time in your life (oftentimes, a specific song can alter your mood in an instant) or remember something fun from your childhood. I think you get the point.
- And speaking of thinking, "you are what you think about" is probably one of the truest statements I have ever heard. If you think negative, your body will project negativity, your eyes will look sad, and the tone of your words will sound defeated. Stop it. When you think about good things, you will notice your eyes light up, you will walk more erect with your head held high, and your

voice will sound inviting to hear. Think about this: Who would you rather hear from? Someone with negativity or someone with positivity? Now put yourself in your customers' place—who do you think they want to hear from?

- If you hang around with turkeys…grow some wings and fly away. Get with the Eagles (love their music), soaring with the clouds. Choose wisely in terms of the coworkers you associate with.
- Here's an idea: instead of having lunch with a negative coworker, go and read a chapter of a book while you eat—improve yourself.
- Constantly read; listen to CDs (not music) while you drive. You will be amazed at how many things your brain can absorb even if you are not listening intently. Some folks actually learn a new language by playing CDs while they sleep. Wow! If you listen to a motivational or sales CD over and over, you will pick up ideas, which you can use during your next sales appointment. I like to call this reinforcement Constant Incremental Improvement (CII).
- Buy and read (or get the CD) *Eat That Frog* by Brian Tracy. But only if you want to get better at managing your time and setting and exceeding goals. Your choice. My recommendation—don't stay stuck.
- Set and track your personal goals, even if you don't read *Eat That Frog*. How in the world do you know how you are doing unless you measure your progress? I know of a sales rep who had a goal of "seven thousand Saturdays"—his goal was to sell $7,000 worth of home-improvement products every Saturday, even if he was given zero appointments. How could he accomplish this with zero appointments? He would self-generate one or two appointments on his own for every Saturday. All he knew was that he had to make his goal, and if it took a little extra work, so be it. As if you couldn't guess, he was one of the top-performing sales reps in the company. Go figure.

Takeaway Nugget(s) from Element 1:

ELEMENT 2

PREPARATION

Here's a clue from professional athletes: you *Must* practice to be a winner! Before a season starts, athletes go through countless hours or days or weeks of practice. Then they have exhibition games. Then, and only then, do they begin their season. So why do you think you can "wing it" during a sales presentation?

- Practice; Practice; Practice!
  - Do your presentation in front of a mirror—see what customers will be seeing.
  - Give your presentation to your spouse, your best friend, and several coworkers. It's OK if you are nervous. Better to lose the jitters when it doesn't count. And they will probably have good feedback for you. Thin skin? Get over it.
  - If someone were to ask me what is the best way to practice, my answer would always be the same: *videotape your presentation*. Is this scary? You bet. Are you nervous? Of course. But after numerous tapings of yourself, you will get better. And if you want the real feedback, watch the tape with your sales manager and sales team. Ask for their candid comments. I know that even though some of their words may be hard to accept, adjusting your presentation will help you in the long run. Try it; you'll like it.

- o Always look for answers to the same two questions after every presentation, whether practicing or "live":
  1. What did I do well?
  2. What could I do better?
- Know your product. And if you can't answer a question, say so and promise to find out the answer at a later time. Most importantly, *do not lie.* To paraphrase a line from the movie *A League of Their Own* (there's no crying in baseball), "There's no lying in sales"—never, ever.
- Always think in terms of "when" and not "if." By using the word "when," you are implying and believing that something *will* happen, not *might* happen. This change in your outlook can have an amazing impact on your sales results and ultimately your life and family.

Muscle Memory: You've probably heard of the Blue Angels. What you may not know about them is that they fly two practice sessions each day, six days per week. Why? They develop muscle memory that allows them to fly within eighteen inches of each other. They have a disciplined execution. If they have a hurricane near Pensacola, Florida, where they are based, and they can't fly for a few days, they have to relearn the muscle memory by practicing for a couple of weeks before they can perform in another air show. You, too, must develop a disciplined execution with your presentation, practicing until it becomes second nature and your brain's muscle memory takes over.

And if you are afraid of rejection, get over it—or find a new profession. If you are an excellent sales rep who closes 50 percent of your appointments, you are still being rejected half of the time!

Listen Up!

- If you are a manager of a sales team, you should be running appointments with each of your reps. I know it will be hard, but you must try not to take over the appointment, even if it is going sideways. The only way they can learn is by doing, and yes, sometimes failing. Before the appointment, in the car (windshield time), review the elements of the presentation together. After the appointment, debrief, letting the sales reps speak first, sharing (1) what they did well and (2) what they could have done better. Focus on the positive, not on the negative. These are teaching moments!

- If you are the sales rep, ask your sales manager to ride with you (you may have to pick him or her off the floor because they will not be expecting this). Also, ask to go on a "joint" appointment with another sales rep at least two times per month. Why? (1) So you can get feedback. (2) Statistically, for commissioned sales reps, closing ratios go up because each sales rep keeps the other on point and can fill in if something is about to be skipped. (3) Sales overage increases because the commission typically needs to be split, and sales reps naturally work harder for the extra commission so their share is higher.

- How long should a presentation be? My answer is always, as long as it needs to be. Make sure you take your time. And if your customers say that their time is limited, just ask for a couple more minutes, and you will usually get an affirmative reply (sometimes my couple more minutes would turn out to be just like the last two minutes of a football game—thirty minutes?). Experienced sales reps will share with you that the longer you are with customers, the more likely you will be able to answer all of their questions, overcome their objections, and ultimately get the sale. Sometimes customers get fatigued by the length of the presentation and eventually say yes to you. Isn't that a good thing?

- If you are on an appointment in the home, and customers ask if you would like to have some dinner or dessert with them, by all means, say *Yes!* This is a clear sign that they like you, and it might be perceived as rude if you say no. There are exceptions to their invitations that should go without saying but need to be said anyway: you should always say no to an offer of a cigarette, a beer, or any other "items" that may be perceived as inappropriate. I hope you don't need any further explanation of this last part.

- And if you are on a B-to-B appointment, and your client asks you if you have time for lunch or dinner (or even breakfast), your answer should always be *Yes!* More face time with a client, especially in a more relaxed setting, is always a good thing. You both will get to know each other better, and this usually leads to liking and trusting each other. Just be careful of your alcohol intake. Slow and easy.

Takeaway Nugget(s) from Element 2:

_____

_____

ELEMENT 3

BE REAL

I'm sure you know who Johnny Cash is. If you saw the movie *Walk the Line*, you may remember the following: Johnny wanted to sing songs more than anything, so he and his two band mates went to the Sun Records Studio in Memphis to record a song. They began to play a gospel song, and Sam Phillips, the producer, stopped them. He said, "Sing something different, something real, something you felt." And then he shared with Johnny that "it has to do with believing in yourself." Johnny then sang a song that he'd written while in the Air Force: "Folsom Prison Blues." Well, I guess Sam Phillips really liked the song because he recorded it and released it, and the rest is history. The moral of this story is you must be real, and you must believe in yourself in order to succeed—in sales and in life.

- If it's an in-home appointment, when you arrive, park on the street. You don't want to know how much it costs to remove oil-leak stains from a driveway. Be considerate.
- If it's B-to-B appointment, be sure to park in a visitor's space. The last thing you want to do is park in someone's designated parking space or create your own parking space in an unauthorized area (or even worse, a handicap parking space).
- Be yourself; be confident. Remember, people buy from **CONFIDENT** people they **LIKE** and **TRUST**.

- When approaching a front door, remember, friends always knock and strangers ring doorbells. Makes sense? Which do you want to be?
- Anyone's first impression of you is made in the blink of an eye. Sorry if you thought you had a few seconds or a minute. So... practice your greeting because it can lead to success or failure.
- When you are at the customers' home for the first time and they open the door, take a step back. If you are a rather tall individual, I recommend you take a step back and a step down to be more at their eye level.
- Space invasion: This is when you physically get or stand too close to people. You should always be mindful of this anytime you are with anyone. This is more important if the other person is of the opposite sex. The last thing you want to do is make your customer uncomfortable with you from the very beginning. Initially, I would recommend being three feet, or an arm's length, away from them. This also makes it easy for the handshake.
- First names: Ask customers permission if you can address them by their first names, and frequently use their names during the presentation. THIS IS VERY IMPORTANT. People like to be called by their name, and it helps in establishing a relationship with your customers. Also, using first names can be an attention getter. We learned this in grade school: remember when a teacher called out your name—and you looked up? And today, if someone calls out your name when you are walking in a shopping mall, don't you instinctively look to see who it is, even if that person is not really calling for you? More about this later.
- Dress professional—not sure I need to elaborate on this. See the previous statement about customers' first impressions.
- No hats. No pens or anything else on your ear—you get a big *c'mon man* if you violate this.
- If you are entering the customers' home, always wipe your feet before you enter. If you want to really score points, ask if they would like you to remove your shoes. Believe me, very few homeowners will say yes, but they will certainly appreciate your respect for their home. This is differentiation at its best. And, yes, I have

to say it: if you make the offer, please ensure you *do not* have a hole in one of your socks. Think about their reaction to the sight of an uncovered big toe!

- No cell phones: Do everyone a favor and leave your cell phone somewhere that you won't be tempted to answer it or even look at it. Besides being annoying, it is downright rude!

- When you shake hands, make it a normal handshake. Don't get cute, and don't squeeze tight. A normal handshake is expected; anything else could lead to a negative judgment, and possibly pain.

- Smiling (or better yet laughter) is always a good sign in the sales process. You should practice smiling, and your goal should be to get your customers to smile and laugh. Telling jokes is OK, but they must be tasteful. Good sales reps use the same "tired" jokes every time. I guess their logic is that these customers are hearing the jokes for the first time.

- Smiling is contagious: Did you ever notice that when you smile at a baby, they naturally smile back? Same goes with adults. If you are not a believer, try this: the next time you go to a grocery store, and you happen to make eye contact with some people, flash them a smile. I bet you will be surprised at the number of smiles you will receive in return.

- If it's an in-home presentation, what should you initially bring into the home? Depending on who you ask, you will get a variety of different answers to this. I would recommend a clipboard with paper on which you can take notes and your two "slim" binders, one with your company story and the other with competitive information (or your laptop with these loaded). More about how or when to use these two binders later. And carry everything in your left hand so you can easily shake hands using your right hand.

- If you are going to a B-to-B meeting, you should arrive with the following:
  - Your presentation (either printed or on a laptop) ready to go without typos and errors. Translation—proofread it ahead of time. At least twice.

- o Written goals for your presentation—to keep you on track.
- o Questions you want to get answers to—and these usually support your goals.
- o A notepad to take notes.
- o An open mind. You never know where the meeting may lead.

Takeaway Nugget(s) from Element 3:

ELEMENT 4

WARM UP (GETTING TO KNOW YOU)

S o, once you are alone with your customers, how do you begin the warm up?

First, if you are on an in-home appointment, you will want to sit in a more casual area of the home—the family room or the living room. Remember to let the homeowners sit down first. How embarrassing would it be if you sat in Mr. Customer's recliner, and he could not sit in his favorite seat? He probably won't say a word but will remember what you did. It could leave a bad taste in his mouth.

If it's a B-to-B appointment, your goal is to get your client out from behind the desk and into a more user-friendly atmosphere. A side table in his or her office would also be good. Or perhaps a conference room. End result: You do not want the desk or table to be a barrier. Let your client choose his or her seat, and preferably sit close to your client (e.g., at the corners of a table) so that you can effectively present. Remember, not too close that you are invading his or her space.

Next, the best way is to follow a simple plan. Always use the acronym FORM (if you know me, you would know I love to use acronyms): Family, Occupation, Recreation, My purpose. People love to talk about themselves, and your goal is to get the conversation going. Caution: *Do not* talk about yourself. If you do, the conversation will likely stall, because customers are truly not interested in you. Someone once told me that after your presentation is over, the only thing customers should know about you is your name. Now that may seem a bit drastic, but you get the point. Focus on them.

- **F**amily: Ask questions about their family; look for clues like pictures on the wall or a table. "How big is your family?" has always worked for me.
- **O**ccupation: Asking a question like "Where do you work?"—although very generic—always gets you an answer that you can build upon for more questions. Obviously, you should skip this question for a B-to-B client.
- **R**ecreation: "What do you like to do when you are not working?" is a great question here. This is the best place to gather insights about your customer and can lead to many "branching" questions that you can ask later on during your presentation.

For each of these three parts of FORM, make sure you ask more than one question. Recommend that you practice the art of using "branching questions"—questions that are follow-ups to the answers they gave to your previous question. More on this soon. Again, you must refrain from giving any information about yourself or, worse yet, telling any stories about yourself.

The last part of FORM is "**M**y purpose." Simply explain that you will:

1. Listen to the needs of your customers. (Forgive me if I am preaching here, but a great sales rep should develop *outstanding listening skills*. Whenever you ask a question, wait for your customers to reply, and make sure they are finished speaking. I would recommend allowing a pause after you think they are finished, just in case they do have something else to add. Remember, you have two ears and one mouth—so human beings, by design, should listen twice as much as they speak.)
2. Share some information about your company.

3. Share your products or services and how these can provide solutions to the needs of your customers.

4. Ask for the order (I know that this can be hard to do, but you *must* let your customers know that this is your plan). No surprises. And then you should state, "If you like what you see, and trust us to do the work, then why not go ahead with the order today? If not, that's OK too. We can shake hands and part as friends, fair enough?" These words will let customers know that it is OK to say no. I've even said to customers that if my product or service is not right for them or their situation, I will say NO for them.

- Share versus tell: If you want to get answers or information from customers (and this also works for your family, especially children), eliminate the use of the word "tell" and begin using "share." Here's why (taking you on a trip down memory lane):
  - When you were in the first grade, and you "told" on one of the other kids, you probably remember being called a tattletale (snitch, narc, etc. can also be substituted), and you didn't like being called that. And you remembered that negative experience.
  - When you were young, your mother probably said to you when other kids were coming over to play that it would be good to share your toys with them, so that when you went to their house, they would do the same. This positive reinforcement led you to believe that sharing was a good thing and that it brought good returns.
  - So, now it's present day, and if people ask you to "tell" them something, in a millisecond, your brain remembers that telling does not bring good memories, and so you are reluctant to tell. Conversely, if you are asked to "share," you remember that sharing is good, and it's OK to go ahead. Make sense? Go ahead and try it—I guarantee you that you will like the results.
  - As an example from first-hand experience in rehashing appointments (a less-than-good way of saying I was calling customers to find out what happened on the appointment) that were already run but not sold, I experimented with the

word "share" versus "tell." When I asked homeowners to "tell" me who they chose to do business with and what they paid, they shut me down, refusing to answer, and they immediately tried to end the phone call. But when I used the word "share," they began to warm up (guess they thought of their own mothers' words) and provided me with competitors' names, prices, and even why they made the decision to do business with them. Sometimes it's the smallest change in words you use that can make the biggest difference. It's also known as wordsmithing.

- Branching questions: As mentioned earlier, these are used to get people to have an extended conversation with you or share more about themselves and their needs. During the warm-up, this type of bonding is very important. It can assist in getting the customers to like and trust you. Branching questions can also be used in Element 9—The Investment. Here are a couple of examples of using branching questions:
  - Good branching question examples: You are sitting in the living room, and on the way in, you see a picture of Mr. Customer holding a big fish.

Q. Are you a fisherman?
A. Well, yes I am. Do you fish?
Q. Yes, I do. What type of fish do you like to catch?
A. Walleye and pike.
Q. Where do you like to fish?
A. I particularly like the Great Lakes.
Q. How many times a year are you able to go fishing?
A. A couple of times a year, some of my buddies and I get together and go for a weekend up north. Usually in the spring and fall.
Q. What type of bait do you use?
A. We usually use lures. We make them ourselves.
Q. How long does it take you to make a lure?
A. On average, around two hours. I like to take my time and make it right.

Q. Do you ever sell any of your lures?
A. No, but I do frequently give them as gifts.
Q. Do any other members of your family like to fish?
A. My two daughters don't like to fish, but just this year, one of my sons-in-law and I went fishing. We had a great time and plan to do it every year.
Q. Do your daughters live here in town?
A. One of my daughters does. The other lives in Cleveland, not too far.

As you can see, I used fishing questions at first and then eventually branched to his daughters. This would allow me to get Mrs. Customer involved in the conversation as well.

- ○ Bad branching question example (this was me before I learned how to use branching questions):

  Q. Are you a fisherman?
  A. Well, yes I am. Do you fish?
  My answer back: "Well, I do all of my fishing at Krogers (a local grocery store). I find I am always able to catch exactly what I need." With this reply, he gave me a startled look, and I knew that my bonding time with him was over.

- ○ Another bad branching question example:

  Q. Are you a fisherman?
  A. Well, yes I am. Do you fish?
  Your answer back: Yes, I like to fish a lot. My favorite place to fish is Winton Woods Lake. I like to go there early in the morning. My favorite bait is baloney, and I usually catch several fish before noon. There are a couple of special spots on the lake that are especially good if you like bluegill.

  If you look up and see your customer's eyes glazed over, it's because he or she doesn't want to hear your story and doesn't care.

You must learn to minimize talking about yourself and your life. Focus on the customer!

- At this point, after you have completed FORM, if your presentation is in the home, you should ask the homeowners if it's OK to move to the kitchen (or dining-room) table, as you will need more room for your presentation. Again, let the homeowners take their seats first. Now, this is very important: you do not want them sitting on one side of the table and you on the other. The table becomes a barrier that you want to avoid if at all possible. This is the best seating arrangement: you on one side of the table, one homeowner on the end of the table, and the other homeowner opposite you. This forms a U shape, which makes for a more interactive presentation. And, if at all possible, if you are male, you don't want Mrs. Homeowner sitting next to you. This could be awkward for Mr. Homeowner, which also makes it uncomfortable for you. In situations like this, I have gently asked them to switch their seats and don't recall ever receiving a refusal. If there is only one homeowner, you do not want him or her to sit across from you; you would want him or her to sit near you—but you should leave a little additional space between you.

Takeaway Nugget(s) from Element 4:

_____

_____

ELEMENT 5

NEADS ANALYSIS (SOLUTION SELLING)

S olution selling is an excellent way to connect with customers. Unless you know what they need (are you clairvoyant?), you cannot offer solutions. By using the NEADS Analysis, you are asking the customers a lot of questions, which will assist you in getting the customers happily involved with your products or services and business. Here's the process:

- **N** = Now. What do the customers have now? If you are selling home-improvement products in the home, you can find out additional information by doing an inspection and taking measurements. Be sure to point out any issues you may observe, and ask a lot of questions.
- **E** = Enjoy. What do the customers enjoy or like about what they have now? Don't be surprised if they tell you they don't like anything about what they have now. That's why they are meeting with you. If they do share some of the features they like, take notes. Especially if you also have those options.
- **A** = Alter or change. What would the customers alter or change? I am sure customers will be more than willing to share their thoughts and ideas. Take notes. If in the unlikely event they don't say anything, then ask them, "If you could wave a magic

wand over what you have, what would you like to change?" This almost always gets you an answer.

- **D** = Decision maker. Who is making the decision? Are all the decision makers present? If not, you need to identify who is missing. You still need to complete the presentation, but understand that you may have to present again during a follow-up meeting. It's also OK to ask, "If you like what you see today, and it fits your needs, would you consider saying yes and moving forward with the project?" During your entire visit or presentation, it is important to get as many yeses as possible. Doing this puts customers in a positive mood and can help you to get the big *Yes* later on.

- **S** = Solutions. Now is the time to narrow down the "wish list." Find out what the most important things are for your customers. Try this: make a list of top ten reasons people have purchased your product or service, and share a copy of the list with each customer (it is very important that each customer does this without any assistance from the other customer). Ask the customers to circle their top three (without looking at the other's answers) and then compare and review the answers. This exercise usually points out what you need to focus on during the rest of your presentation and may get both customers on the same page.

It is important during the NEADS analysis that the topic of the "runaround" (i.e., when customers call a company for issues, parts, and/or services and they are told they need to call someone else) is covered. If the customers don't bring it up, then you need to ask them the following question: "Have you ever experienced the runaround?" If they say yes, ask them to share their story. And then listen to everything they say. This will undoubtedly help you later on. If they've never heard of the runaround, then be prepared to share with them a story from one of your other customers. *Never* share with them a runaround experience you had. It's more believable if it's a story from another customer.

Very Important: The basis for your entire presentation should be question-based selling—always ask a lot of questions, and let the customers take their time to reply. This is the best way to find out what customers are thinking—their feelings and emotions. Or, instead of asking questions, you can keep talking and accept your poor sales results—up to you. (I suggest if you are interested in improving your sales numbers, there is a book out there called *Secrets of Question Based Selling* by Thomas A. Freeze).

OK. The next elements are where the Value Blocks can really be seen by your customers. Don't take shortcuts. You have practiced your presentation so many times that it should be easy to share it one more time. And most importantly, have fun, because now: IT'S SHOWTIME!

Takeaway Nugget(s) from Element 5:

ELEMENT 6

COMPANY INFORMATION

Y ou should have your company information presentation either in a flip binder or on a laptop. Be careful not to have too many pages, if it's in a binder—it may scare your customers. And *never* say, "Well, it looks like a lot, but I'll skip most of it"—because they will be thinking, "Well, why is it there in the first place, if you are going to skip it?"

What are the components of a good company story?

- A little history of the company with important dates in bullet points—don't over elaborate. Talk about the people who work for your company. How proud you are to be representing your company.
- Company mission, values, and guiding principles, if your company has them. Let your customers see them and read them. It makes them real.
- BBB status. Have a printed copy of your company's BBB status that you can show, and make sure it's current. A dated copy suggests you have something to hide. If you do have some complaints, put them into perspective. For example, if your company has five complaints (and let your customers know that all complaints have been resolved, if they have) and does fifteen hundred installations a year, do the math for them. That's 0.3 percent (one-third of 1 percent) of customers. Said in a positive

way, 99.7 percent of customers have had a good experience with us. Now for a tie-down question—"Is this the type of company you would like to do business with?"

- Insurance coverage that customers should be interested in, such as workers' comp and liability. And show them copies of the current policies. You *cannot* have outdated copies and just say there are new policies in force. Would you believe you?

- If doing an installation, explain to your customers if your installers are company employees or subcontractors, and explain why. *Do not* lie to customers about this, or it could cost you the sale and undoubtedly future referrals. If your company uses subcontractors, and they ask you about this, you could say: "Yes, we do use subcontractors, just like the builder who built your home. But what you are really asking is who stands behind our products. The real difference is that if you have a product or service issue, you only need to call us so we can take care of your issue. As I mentioned before, no runaround."

- If you use employee installers, let your customers know if they are drug tested, background checked, and bonded. Good things.

- Industry ratings of your products. Briefly explain how the ratings work and how proud you are of the ratings your products earned. Be able to share specific ratings if requested to do so.

- Industry associations. Briefly describe industry associations and how they are important to your customers. The easiest way is to display all the logos on one page (point to them with a pen and describe them).

- Awards. Briefly share with your customer any outstanding or noteworthy awards earned by your company (e.g., BBB award for customer ethics).

- Testimonials. I would recommend you carry with you copies of some of your best testimonials, written by homeowners. How do you share these with your customers? Prepare your testimonials by highlighting in yellow (the easiest-on-the-eyes highlight color) the important phrases or sentences of your testimonials. Keep them in plastic pages, and take them out and hand them to the customers. Ask them to only read the highlighted parts.

Remember, you should alternate handing one to Mr. Customer and then one to Mrs. Customer, keeping both of them involved in the process. Again, take your time with this part of your presentation: go at their pace. Your previous customers are now helping you to make this sale with their words. We'll discuss the process of getting testimonials a little later on. And if you are a new sales rep, borrow some testimonials from other reps until you build a bank of your own.

- When you are finished with your company story, another tie-down question. Does *Company Name* seem like the type of company you would like to do your *name the product or service* with?

Under the category of Always Be Prepared, you should have a competitive information (CI) binder (a completely separate binder) that you can refer to, as needed. Use this info only if you have to—to answer a question or make a point. Customers *do not* like it when sales reps "bad-mouth" the competition. Your CI binder should contain the following on your major competitors (and yes, it's an unacceptable excuse if you don't have this because you think it's too hard to compile—remember, Turkey or Eagle?):

- Product brochures.
- Current industry ratings.
- Current BBB status.
- Copies of warranties.
- Copies of recent competitor sales quotes—provided to you by customers who chose to do business with you and not your competitor.
- Samples—I know some sales reps who actually carry real samples of their competitors' products with them to overcome the objection by the customers that they still want to see the competitors' products. More about this later.

Takeaway Nugget(s) from Element 6:

ELEMENT 7

PRODUCT INFORMATION

W hen you get to this part of your presentation, if you have samples of your products in your car (if it's an in-home presentation), excuse yourself with your customers, stating that you need to get a couple of important things to show them. During your trip to the car, talk to yourself, reminding yourself that this is the part where you can really excel. And when you are outside, they will be able to talk to each other about you and how much they like and trust you. When you get back to the door, again, wipe your feet.

MORE SHOWTIME!

- Rev up your excitement.
- Elevate your voice, but don't yell.
- Sit down and present your product—do not stand. Customers don't like anyone to be standing when they are sitting. It also, literally, can give customers a pain in the neck by constantly having to look up at you from their seated position.
- Always say that you would like to "share" your product, not "show," because show always goes along with "tell," and that's not good.
- Walk them through the Features, Advantages, and Benefits (FAB) of your products or services. Make sure you use an example they could be familiar with, like the following:
  - Feature: Cup holders in the console of a car.

- o   Advantage: Your console offers four cup holders, two of which are self-adjusting to hold different sizes of cups.
- o   Benefit: Safety and cleanliness, for example, minimizes hot coffee spills.
- Is there anything you have for them to hold or anything you can ask them to rate as you go through the presentation? If you are using a device that gives ratings or numbers (e.g., a glass demonstration for window sales reps), have a form ready for them to fill out. As you slide the form halfway across the table, ask, "Could one of you provide an assist by filling in the numbers as we go?" *Hint: more often than not, your decision maker will be the one who reaches for the form and agrees to help.*
- Take your time—explain.
- Ask if they have any questions after every segment—and answer them.
- Confirm their responses—"So...what you like about this is..." "So...what I heard you say was..."
- Before and after pictures: If you are selling products that can have before and after pictures (such as home improvement), do yourself a favor and have a few examples available. You can use these as price conditioners. Here's how. Share that you have a few examples of your existing customers' projects. Show one of the before pictures first, asking them what they believe this home would sell for as shown? Then show them the after picture and ask them the same question. Do the math for them, and share how much the home has appreciated since completion of the project. Repeat this process one or two more times, but stop once you have made your point. The amount of appreciation of value has always exceeded the final investment for the homeowners whom I have used this with. And I was always using their numbers, not mine. This is a very important step that a lot of sales reps exclude in the interest of time. Don't take the shortcut.
- Once you are finished with your Product Information section, ask the tie-down question—"Is this the type of product you would like to have for your home?" Obviously, you would like a *Yes* answer to this question. If customers say no, you need to find out

why, perhaps saying, "Why do you say that?" Give them time to answer. They may take a minute to reply, and then your goal is to overcome their objection before moving on.

- CI and competitor actual samples: If their objection is competitor related, like, "We haven't seen the ABC and/or XYZ product yet," then this is where your CI binder can be of assistance in overcoming the objection. You could start with competitors' brochures, but better yet, if you have some of your competitors' samples with you, you could suggest that they "go shopping" by looking at the competitors' samples you have. You're probably asking, "Where can I get samples of my competitors' products?" Here's where:
  - From your installers who have removed your competitor's product when replacing with your product.
  - From your competitor—without identifying yourself as a sales rep of a competitor, purchase the product directly.
  - If it's home-improvement products like windows or doors, your competitor may have donated excess products to Habitat for Humanity. It would be worth the trip to go and see.
  - *Do not* go "Dumpster diving" at your competitor's location, as it is both illegal and dangerous. Use one of the other methods listed above. Don't risk your life or your reputation.

The most important thing to remember is that you are not selling a commodity. You are selling yourself, your company, and your product or service—and there are a lot of important differences between what they are seeing now and what is available in the marketplace. *Build your value!*

Takeaway Nugget(s) from Element 7:

ELEMENT 8

TRIAL-CLOSES

Trial-close questions (a.k.a. tie-downs) should be asked by you after very section of your visit or presentation. Don't you want to know what the customers are thinking about you, your company, and your product or service all along the way? Their answers can provide you cues and clues you can use during your sharing of the investment and negotiation.

One of the Most Important Parts of This Book You Need to Learn—The Four Questions

After the product or service presentation, and before you begin to share the investment and negotiate, here are the questions you *must* use:

1. Is this the *type* of product or service you would like to have? (do not say *is this the product*, because they may answer they don't know as they are still shopping). You want a YES answer to this question.
2. Would you buy a lesser-grade product or service even if it were a cheaper price? You want a NO answer to this question.
3. Setting aside the money (I have even added "let's put the money in the other room, up on a shelf in the closet, and close the closet door and the door to the room"), if money were not part of the decision, would you like this product or service? You want a YES answer to this question.

4. So, if I could make this product or service 100 percent affordable for your budget, is there any other reason why you could not move forward with your decision while we are together today? You want a NO answer to this question. This is a critical time. You are attempting to get tie-downs on your product or service and company and their willingness to make a decision. If they do have objections, this is where they will usually share them. You need to overcome *all* of their objections before moving on.

*   Measure your customers' reactions to these questions, and watch their body language for clues and cues.
*   If their only objection is "Well, we might be able to make a decision, but we haven't seen your price," your reply should be "Great. The investment part of my presentation is next, so let's move on to it, fair enough?"

Takeaway Nugget(s) from Element 8:

_____

_____

THE INVESTMENT (A.K.A. NEGOTIATING)

W hy are most products and services negotiated? Negotiating is the one thing customers hate doing the most, but it is also expected, and often demanded, by customers. Some companies tried to eliminate negotiating (Saturn cars) and sales (J. C. Penney), but consumers did not respond favorably. I guess that since we were young, we learned that negotiations are an expected part of life.

For you, as a sales rep, there are some important things to remember:

- When you are presenting the investment, you should always ask for more than you need, because it leaves you room to negotiate, and the customers may just say yes.
- No one likes to "buy" a product or service without getting something in return. It usually is an investment in a certain feature, advantage, or benefit that is the convincing factor: for example, a flavor, the presentation, a color. The ultimate goal in any sale is for all parties (your customers, you, and your company) to be happy with the final result. Providing a good return on the investment (ROI) is the ticket to success. Give the customers a reason to make the investment you are asking for.

- *Always* refrain from using the words "price" and "cost" when you refer to your products or services. These words have negative connotations for consumers (but it's OK to use these words when speaking of your competitors' products or services). Use the word "investment" instead. It implies that they will get something other than just the product or service for their money.

Stop me if you've heard this one. Two brothers need to go with you on every customer appointment or meeting: twins ERBN and LRBN. Notice they have the same last name (RBN) but different first names. Their full names are *Emotional* Reasons for Buying Now and *Logical* Reasons for Buying Now. For you see, if you don't bring both brothers with you, you may not only lose the sale but may have a sale canceled on you the next day. Here's why. Customers can be swayed by their emotions when it comes to you, your company, your product demo, and even your promotional "price" (yes, I used the word, but only for effect). But the next day, someone else (friend, coworker, relative, neighbor, etc.) may suggest to them that they could have gotten "a better deal" elsewhere. Since you have not provided them with the logical reasons for their decision, they may rethink their decision, and then they call to put the sale on hold or even cancel. But if you shared the logic of your product, its value, and even its ROI (return on investment), they will probably defend their purchasing decision and perhaps even suggest to the naysayer that they should call you if they have a need for your products. So, remember to take brothers ERBN and LRBN with you every time. Don't leave home without them!

More negotiating tips:

- Focus on financing: Monthly payments will fit into customers' budgets much easier than paying cash. When is the last time you or someone you know bought a new car or a house with cash? That's what I'm talking about. And homeowners are used to making monthly payments for gas and electric, cable or dish TV, telephone, insurances, and so on. Help them by putting this into perspective. They will appreciate your assistance in purchasing the product or service they really want.

- Don't use round numbers; use odd numbers. For example, if the investment comes to $1,000, use $999 or $989 as you are presenting three numbers instead of four. Why do you think grocery stores offer two products for $0.99 instead of two for $1.00? Buyer perception is they are paying less.

- Reduce to ridiculous: Car sales reps are taught this, and you probably experienced it when buying a car. Instead of talking about the sticker price of the car, they want to get to the payment amount you can afford. So, if it's a $30,000 car, and you have a $4,000 trade in (or down payment), with 0 percent financing for five years, the monthly payment would be $433.33 ($26,000 divided by sixty months). But why stop there? If you divide the monthly payment amount of $433.33 by an average of thirty days in a month, your payment per day would be $14.44. What if you factor in the mileage driven per day? If their daily commute is twenty miles one way, that's forty miles per day. Now their daily investment is only $0.36 per mile. And the gas mileage and reduced maintenance they will get from their new vehicle haven't even been factored in! Help your customers to understand the effective investment in light of their enjoyment, and they will undoubtedly help you to make the sale by saying *Yes.*

  Your next assignment: develop this type of example for your product or service and incorporate it into your selling process. Good selling! You're welcome.

- Using a calculator: You should *always* use a calculator to do your calculations and check your numbers (remember, measure twice, cut once). Show your customers the numbers on the calculator. This makes the numbers real.
  - Your calculator should be the size that can fit into your pocket.
  - Put your calculator away after every calculation—this says to your customers that there are no more calculations to make (or discounts to give).

- ○ If customers question your calculations, happily redo them. Do not argue that your numbers are right.
- Write subsequent offers using smaller numbers: As you go through your negotiating process, you may be providing additional discounts off your initial investment amount. When you are writing the numbers down, your first number should be written in a normal size. Each subsequent investment number you write down should be smaller in size than the previous number. This reinforces to your customers that the numbers are getting smaller (a.k.a. funneling), both in amount and in size. What you are subliminally demonstrating is that that it's getting closer to the time when the numbers cannot get any smaller either in the amount or in size. The negotiating is essentially over. Tick tock. It's time to make a decision.
- "Quid pro quo"—this is usually recognized as a legal term: I will give you something if you give me something in return. Any reduction in the original investment *must be justified* by getting the customers to agree to also give something.
  - ○ A great tactic to use for this is a Marketing Agreement. Design a form that includes some things they can do for you for an additional discount:
    - ▪ Provide two referrals (or more).
    - ▪ Write a testimonial letter.
    - ▪ Agree to let other customers talk to them about their experience.
    - ▪ Put a sign in their yard (if it's a home-improvement project).
    - ▪ Anything else specific to your industry.
  - ○ Have them check boxes next to the items they agree to do.
  - ○ The Marketing Agreement must have a signature line for the customer to sign—that makes it real.
  - ○ If you haven't already figured it out, the two key items you want them to agree to are the referrals and the testimonial letter.
  - ○ Share with them how easy it is to provide two referrals— from their pool of family, friends, coworkers, relatives, and neighbors.

- End of the month: Everybody knows that companies are always hustling to hit their monthly sales goals. Use this to your advantage. Mention that if your customers can say yes to the product or service, they would be eligible for the end-of-month special—but only if they make a buying decision before the end of the month.
- Price increase: Companies usually, at regular intervals, have price increases. If one is on the horizon, let your customers know this so that they can take advantage of the savings—but only if they make a buying decision before the price increase goes into effect.
- Don't use "choose two": Don't let your customers select which two of the following they want: speed, quality, or price. Because they will say they want all three, and then you will spend a lot of time explaining why you can't provide one of the three. This is one tactic that is best left unused.
- Higher authority: If your customers are having difficulty making a decision, you can try the higher authority technique. You could say: "If you folks are serious about moving forward with this product or service, and are ready to say yes, I can make a call to my manager, and perhaps he or she will authorize a one-time special discount. Are you ready to say yes?" Very important: you *must* get their agreement to this before you make the call.
  - Customers can also use the higher authority as an excuse to not make a decision. They will say that they will need to speak with their spouse, another relative, or perhaps a friend before they can make a decision. What you need to do is get them to possibly contact that person while you are there. But, before you do this, you need to say the following to your customer: "I understand how you feel. But let me ask you this. If that person walked through the door right now, what would you share about my product, what you like, and also, what would you recommend regarding moving forward with this project?" Your goal is to get the customers to express their feelings to you (hopefully positive) before they speak with their higher authority. Again, you need to try to close the sale, so try this. You will be surprised how it can work for you.

- Ask the tough questions: Always try to get your customers to share with you what amount they are expecting to spend for your product or service. If you do not do this, and you provide the first numbers, you could end up negotiating with yourself when they say that your numbers are too high—try again. Try this: "I'm sure that before I arrived for this appointment (or came into the store), you folks discussed this project. What did you think a project like this would run? What did you believe *the product* (*name the specific product*) would be?" After you say these words, *be quiet.* Allow your customers time to think about and provide an answer. Note that I did not use the word "cost" or "price" in the questions, as they connote negativity. You will be amazed at how many customers will actually share their numbers with you.
- Reactions: Reacting to customers' statements or numbers with shock or surprise, either with words or a look (a.k.a. flinching), will let the customers know that it's not possible—for example, you can't agree to their proposal. Seeing you flinch while you say the words is very convincing.
  - Note: Customers may flinch at your proposals. You must know how to respond, by justifying your proposal, referring back to features, advantages, and benefits. Do not show weakness by going quiet and looking down or away, as these are signs of submission and that the customers will probably get their way.
- Don't be confrontational: When people are confronted or feel pressured, the natural reaction is for them to back away, shut down, or, even worse, push back. None of these are beneficial to getting the sale. In sales, influence is your best trait—being able to get customers to put the pressure on themselves, to say yes to your product or service. Make it their decision, not yours!
- "Feel," "felt," "found": These three words can be very valuable to you. If customers say they can't move forward with the project for a particular reason, you could use feel, felt, found as follows: "I understand how you feel. Many of our happy customers initially felt the same way. But after they purchased our product and experienced the benefits I shared with you, they found that

saying yes was one of the best decisions they could have made." Using other people in your example is always effective. Just like testimonials.

- Splitting the difference: I never recommend doing this. If you have a proposal on the table for, say, $9,900, and the customers offer you $8,900, and you have declined that amount, they will probably come back to you with "let's split the difference" for $9,400. You will be tempted to take their offer, making the sale, but you need to say *No*. Here's why—if you say yes, they will wonder how much lower they could have gone where you would have said yes. So they could end up with a bad taste in their mouth. What you should say to their split-the-difference offer is, "Unfortunately I can't do that. But here's what I can do." And then get a quid pro quo for another reduction. For example: "As you know, our business is built on referrals, which represent nearly XX percent of our business. If you could commit to providing me with a couple of referrals after your project is completed, I can reduce the amount by $250 to $9,650. All I need for you to do is fill out this Marketing Agreement, and we can get your paperwork completed." If the customers still want a few more dollars off, perhaps they could agree to do something else on the Marketing Agreement. Now you are at the point where you are negotiating over small dollar amounts, instead of large ones. All subsequent negotiations should be for ever-decreasing amounts. Bottom line: remember you are a fair and reasonable person, and so are your customers. The goal of any negotiation should be to reach a fair and reasonable conclusion.
- Nibbling: This usually comes into play once an agreement is reached.
  - From the customer's side: They might ask for something additional, for free, before they authorize the paperwork. An example of this may be when customers have agreed to purchase a whole house full of windows, and then when you agree on the investment, they say, "But only if you throw in the two garage windows for free." You will probably be tempted to say yes, just to get the project, but you should not. Rather,

you should say something like this: "Unfortunately, you know we cannot do that, but here's what we can do if you want to include the two garage windows." Then suggest that if they can agree to a couple of items on the Marketing Agreement, then perhaps you could provide an additional, smaller discount on the garage windows. Now you are nibbling back. *Do Not* give away anything free, including a storm door, just to get the signature. If you do, you will be devaluing your product, after you have spent a great deal of time building product value. Also, remember, if you give in to their nibble, they will probably try to nibble on you for something else.

○ From your side (again, using a home-improvement example): If you have finally reached an agreement on the house-full-of-windows investment amount, and the customers also need a new entry door based on your inspection, you could suggest that for just a slightly larger investment, they could get the door replaced at the same time. Here is a great way to include this: If they have decided to finance the project (twenty windows for $14,000, with $4,000 initial investment = $10,000 over three years on a 0 percent financing rate = $277.78 per month), let them know what the additional payment amount per month would be to add the entry door and provide a finishing touch to the new look of their home. If the new entry door was $1,800, the additional monthly payment would *only* be $50 per month, or $1.67 per day. How could they not agree to do this?

• Always be ethical: Don't make a deliberate mistake, and try to correct it later by adding more money. If you have seen the movie *Tin Men* (a great movie depicting the unethical side of the home-improvement industry), you will know exactly what I am talking about. Sorry, but if you've made a mistake, own up to it, especially if it is in the customer's favor. And if you reach an agreement, do not try to change the agreement. Remember, if your modus operandi is to be deceptive or unethical, you are mortgaging your future business. In other words, whether they do business with you or not, customers will *Never Recommend* you or your company to anyone, ever. It's not worth it. If you've ever given money back to a homeowner due to a mistake you've made, you know how real their surprise to your honesty was. And rest assured that when they speak to family, friends, coworkers, and neighbors, they will share the story of your honesty. And then be prepared for referrals.

- Take it or leave it: This is an ultimatum, and it usually is never a good thing to use in negotiations and never a good thing for you to say to a customer. Period. Unless you want them to ask you to leave. And if they say these words to you, well, it's time for you to be a diplomat. You have three choices:

  o You can call their bluff, letting them know that, unfortunately, you cannot accept their offer, and begin to pack up your things to depart. This is very risky. You are hoping they will relent and say, "Wait," and then you can negotiate a fair settlement. But if after you leave, you think they will respond to your phone call at a later time, well, "you've got another think coming."

  o You could try to appeal to the one who said, "Take it or leave it," by offering a small counter offer, and saying, "Unfortunately, I cannot accept your offer, but here's what I can do (explain your counter offer); if it's OK with your other half (or spouse or partner), would it be OK with you?" By saying this, you are trying to get the other person to weigh in on the decision. It can and will work, but you will need to practice this.

  o You could try to find a way for your customer to give in just a little bit and not lose face: "I know you really want to move forward, and I would hate to have such a small amount of $____keep you from getting what you want. Let's go ahead and start the paperwork at $____ (your new, slightly less offer), fair enough?" Now you are appealing to their sense of fair play, and you have nothing to lose—you are already at *No*.

- Don't be a hammer: A hammer is a tool (and nobody wants to be a tool) that is usually used to pound things. Don't pound on your customers like a hammer. You should be there as a consultant, to help them find a solution to their needs. Remember, a good negotiator does not convince them to say *yes*; a good negotiator gets the customers to put the pressure on themselves to say *yes* through Emotions and Logic (ERBN and LRBN).

- **EVERYTHING IS NEGOTIABLE**: You must believe this. If this is your mantra, then you will be successful in sales. And you must practice this wherever you go to purchase anything, including grocery stores (you can get discounts on dented canned goods; meat with a date nearing its sell by date, because it is still good, especially if you use it the same day or freeze it; twelve packs of soda that are broken open and missing a can—just find a department manager and ask how much—and if he or she says no, well, you were already at No before you asked). Remember, you have nothing to lose. And yes, gas at a gas station is negotiable—just go to another gas station with cheaper gas!
  - Negotiating when you are shopping is fun, and it is free. And it provides you practice to improve your negotiating skills that you use for sales. Try it; you'll like it.
  - The only things that I believe are non-negotiable are your faith, your integrity, and your love.
- Use the word "let's"—actually this is a contraction of the words "let us." This word should be used in your attempt to get an agreement (by the way, "let's" can be used with your spouse, kids, friends, etc., and this would be a great way to practice your use of this word and see the effectiveness of using it). "So, since you like what you see, let's go ahead and get your order started." "Let's" indicates that you are working together with your customers to reach a solution. It is a proven tactical method in sales to get a *yes*. And remember, you have nothing to lose by using "let's" but a lot to gain.

Final Thought

According to the Rolling Stones (hard to imagine this iconic rock band from the 1960s is still doing concerts), "You can't always get what you want, but if you try sometimes, you just might find, you get what you need."

So, always try to get the sale, but don't be afraid to walk away—especially if it's not a win for you, your customers, and/or your company!

Takeaway Nugget(s) from Element 9:

ELEMENT 10

HANDLING OBJECTIONS

Good sales reps enjoy getting objections because they are always buying signals. You should never fear objections; you should always embrace them. And then overcome them.

- Be compassionate when your customers raise objections. "I understand how you feel. My wife and I also frequently make decisions the same way. Is there perhaps one thing that I could do or say that might allow you to move forward with this project or product or service?" And be prepared to answer their question openly and honestly. At least you have continued the dialogue.
- Ask questions—and lots of them. For example, "Why do you say that?" You always want to know the reasons why someone says something. If you do not seek to understand your customers' reasoning, then you cannot attempt to overcome their objection, and your negotiation, and sale, has probably ended.
- Nice People: If your customers are saying no to your project or product or service but are not providing any objections, you may want to try the "Nice People" tactic. "Mr. and Mrs. Customer, when folks say no to my proposal, it's always for one of two reasons. It's me, my company, or my product (pause here) or the price (OK to use "price" here, because it's bad). Do you have any issues with me (pause to let them answer), my company (again pause), or my product (again pause)?" If they still have issues or questions, you must overcome them or answer to move on. If

they say no, everything is OK with you, your company, and your product, then you need to say, "So if it's the price, what can I do or say that could help you to say yes? Is it the overall investment or the monthly payment that doesn't fit into your budget?" And now you must stay silent and wait for their answer. And respond to their answer.

o   Perhaps you should recommend "dropping the product" (taking away options) to make the investment more favorable. If the customers do not want to do this, then perhaps you can recommend monthly payments (if you have not already offered) or a different payment option (longer term).

o   This is your time to get creative and use something you haven't offered before, like the following:

▪   A gift card: I know of companies that print plastic cards with their logo and a dollar amount to simulate a gift card. It looks just like a "live" credit card, except that it can only be used on the company's products. This card could be used as a last resort discount with customers just before you leave their home or they leave your store. You must remind them that this gift card is for today only and cannot be used at a later time.

o   Another tactic: you could ask the customers what it would take for them to say yes. You may not like their answer, but at least you will know where they stand. Now is the time to, again, employ your negotiating strategies and tactics covered in Element 9.

Here's one final suggestion for you to use to get the sale. This can work, but you have to try it to believe it:

o   After you have reviewed the product or service on the agreement with the customers (and the agreement is in front of them), simply point to where their signatures are required and say, "OK, all we need to do to get this project started in our system is simply sign here." Then lay your pen down in front of them and be quiet. Sometimes all it takes is for you to ask for the order one more time!

- Watch body language (yours and theirs)
  - It is estimated that two-thirds of all communication is done nonverbally!
  - Body language provides keys to a person's feelings—I am sure you remember your mother's "stop that" look. You certainly don't want to be on the receiving end of that look from a customer.
  - When adults tell a lie, their usual reaction is to move a hand to the mouth or another part of the face because that is what they learned at a young age. When kids tell a lie, they usually put their hand over their mouth.
  - Eye contact is very important, especially for women. If you are presenting to a couple, make sure you are looking at each of them for an equal amount of time. If you don't, one of them may cease talking or, even worse, leave the room. By the way, if the female leaves the room, you've most likely lost the decision maker.
  - Finger pointing is one of the worst gestures you could use with customers. At a minimum it comes across as aggressive; at the worst, hostile. If you use finger pointing with customers, they may put you in the rude category, and it might be one of the reasons they say *No* to your proposal.
  - Attention getting: If you are trying to make a point, do not use your fingers. Instead, use a pen to point with. This will show your customers what you want them to focus on. Word of caution: do not use the pen like a conductor leading an orchestra. And remember, there are only so many points you should make during a presentation.

Understand this: Most people are nice, so they will not share with you how they really feel until they invite you to leave (or they leave) without a sale, not providing a legitimate objection. That's their way of saying that you did not connect with them.

- *Never* use the money gesture of rubbing your thumb and fingertips. This gesture is commonly used to denote money and will be offensive to your customers.
- Arms—If you are sitting across from customers and their arms are folded, this means they are not receptive to you or what you are saying or doing. Their arms are a barrier to their open mind. So, how do you get them to "open up?" Simply:
  - Hand them something to look at—anything they have to reach for.
  - Use their name, and ask them a question. Using their name gets their immediate attention and is usually followed up by opening their arms and leaning a bit forward (remember what you did when your name was called out by your teacher in grade school).
  - You *must* get their arms unfolded before you continue with your presentation.
- Hands—Try to always keep your hands in the "palms-up" position as much as you can. Palms up from a customer is an indication they are open to what you are saying or doing. You must also remember to never clench your fists, as this is a sign of being ready to fight. And if your customers' fists are clenched, well, this is not a good sign, and you must immediately try to hand them something. You may need to get creative, but just like folded arms, you cannot continue your presentation until you have gotten the fists to disappear.
- Hands, part two—Look for the "church steeple" sign from customers. This is when they position their hands under their chin like the top of a church. If you see this after you have presented a solution to their needs, this is a positive gesture. You may want to ask for the order! By the way, you should never use the church steeple as it could be perceived as a sign of arrogance.
- Legs and feet—If you are a person who has nervous legs or feet (they are constantly moving up and down), you need to learn

to stop the motions. True story: on an appointment with a sales rep, he presented the investment, and because he was nervous, we felt the results of a "rep-quake." All of us could feel the floor vibrating and see the table moving—all because his nervousness caused his knees and feet to keep bouncing up and down. If you have this issue, you may want to try placing one foot on top of the other. Subliminally, your one foot is telling your other foot to stay in place. This really works, if you need it.

o Heads (customer)—During your presentation, you need to keep an eye on your customers' heads. If you see their:

- heads straight up, they are paying attention. Continue on.

- heads down, they are showing a lack of interest in you or your presentation (or they may be ready to nod off— more about this when we get to boredom). In any case, you need to get back their attention. Use their name and/or try to hand them something.

- heads turned to the side—that is, if they are looking at their spouse—then they may be measuring their interest in you or your product. If they are looking away from you and your presentation, perhaps they are thinking about something else in another room. And if they are sitting in their chair sideways, they may be looking to make an escape. For sure, you need to retrieve their attention.

- heads tilted to the side, which is an interesting pose, it usually demonstrates a keen interest in what someone is seeing or hearing. Continue on. (If you have a dog, you may notice this when he or she is trying to get your attention. Our dog, Scarlet, tilts her head when we say the word "hungry?")

o Head (you)—Head nods, when used subliminally, can be very effective.

- If you are asking a question like "Wouldn't you agree that our product's lifetime warranty is far better than any other in the industry?" you can, very gently, nod your own head yes as you are making this statement. Done correctly, people don't notice you are doing it. And it may cause them to also nod their heads affirmatively.

- If you are asking a question like "Would you want builder-grade products in your home even if they were a cheaper price?" you can, very gently, move your head from side to side, answering your own question with a subliminal no. Again, this may cause people to begin to shake their heads no to mimic what they are seeing.
- **CAUTION**: You must be very careful with using this, for if you are too obvious, they could begin to distrust your attempt at manipulation. If you wish to try this, you *must* practice this. And the best way is to videotape yourself to make sure it is minimally noticeable. If you can't perfect it, you shouldn't use it. It's like a pitcher who tries to throw a curve ball and instead throws a "hanging curve," which is often deposited in the bleacher seats for a home run.

o Boredom—Hopefully this never applies to you. As you already know, customers can get bored during your presentation or visit. Yawning—well, that's an obvious sign. Also, watch to see if they rest their head in their hands, drumming their fingers or fingernails, or they are looking around. If they are doing any of these, then you need to get them reinvolved: ask them a question.

- If they happen to doze off because you are talking too much, you need to get their attention by saying their name, followed by a question. And you need to stop talking so much! (Yes, this really happened.)

o Signs of interest—They are leaning forward, their arms are open, one hand is placed against a cheek but is not supporting the head, they ask a lot of questions, or they reach out and touch your samples. Time to ask for the order!

o Decision-making signals—Are your customers moving their fingers across their chin? They are probably thinking. Are they beginning to talk to each other, asking each other questions? Might be time for you to employ the "Excuse Me" technique.

- "Mr. and Mrs. Customer, it seems to me that you folks would like a little time to talk to each other. Maybe I need to step outside (if you are in their home or step aside if you are in the store or their business—to give them some space). When you are ready for me to return, just give me a signal." Give them some privacy to share their thoughts and ideas with each other.

- "Time is on your side"—Not just a good song by the Rolling Stones. You can use time to your advantage when you are selling:

  ○ Be cautious of your speaking pace. You should never speak faster than your customers can hear. Frequently pause between ideas to take a breath. Pauses are an effective way for you to maintain their attention to what you are saying. And sometimes customers will take advantage of your pause so they can ask you a question.

  ○ The longer you are with customers, the more likely you will get a *Yes* to your product or service.

  ○ Often, customers become decision makers when under some time pressure.

  ○ The longer you are negotiating with customers, the more likely they will see the logic of your reasoning.

  ○ Understand that the longer you are in negotiations, the more likely you will be giving a discount—just to make the sale. But that's OK because a smaller sale is always better than *No Sale*!

  ○ You are investing time and energy into the presentation, and you should always have a goal of leaving with something positive: a sale, a scheduled follow-up, or, at the least, a good impression. While they may not become your customers, they may refer you to someone who could use your products or services sometime in the future.

Be cognizant of the cardinal rule of body language: *When the mind closes, the body follows.*

Takeaway Nugget(s) from Element 10:

ELEMENT 11

PAPERWORK

- Paperwork: I would recommend that you begin to use the word "paperwork" instead of "contract." More wordsmithing. People don't like to sign contracts, but they are OK with authorizing the paperwork. And a written agreement will prevent confusion later on. Remember, people believe what they see in writing! Make sure everything that is agreed to is written down in the agreement and signed by the customers. It is a good business practice to read the specifics of the product or service (e.g., color, the number of units, dates, etc.) and ask them if they have any additional questions before you ask them to authorize the paperwork—this will eliminate issues at installation or delivery.
  - If you have the agreement and there needs to be changes:
    - If the changes are minimal, you could make the changes, and you and the customers should initial the changes.
    - If the changes are excessive, you should rewrite the agreement for new signatures. Why is this important? Because this document becomes binding, and if the agreement is not legible, it could be misinterpreted by your ordering department, preproduction group, installers, or even your customers. You want to make sure everything is completely spelled out and not subject to interpretation. So…if your handwriting is atrocious, you probably need to go back to printing.

    o   And you should know your and your company's position on the cancellation of a product or service. If you go into a customer's home to make a sale, they have a three-day (business days) right of rescission. And this should be stipulated in your paperwork—it's the law. But, sometimes, for a lot of reasons, customers may contact you or your company after three days to cancel. My philosophy has always been: "I do not want to do business with someone who doesn't want to do business with me." And I cancel the project. I learned early on that arguing with customers and getting attorneys involved to try to keep the project going is never worth it. It could cost you more than the profit that was in the project.

A wise man once shared with me "some of the most profitable business is the business you walk away from."

    o   What's your reputation worth? It's *priceless*. Always remember this when you are working with customers.

- Deposits: This should be part of your paperwork. And don't be afraid to ask for it. Usually, products or services are custom designed or manufactured for your customers, so you are entitled to get some money down. (By the way, I would recommend that instead of calling it a down payment, call it an initial investment—more wordsmithing, and it sounds better.) How much should you ask for? Well, if your company wants one-third, I would ask for a 50 percent initial investment, as customers often like to negotiate this (make sure you know your state laws; in some states, you cannot receive more than one-third as an initial investment).

    o   Try these words: "Mr. and Mrs. Customer, with a project of this size, and since it is custom made, we typically get an initial investment of 50 percent (do the calculations on a calculator, multiplying the total investment by 50 percent and showing them the result on the calculator; makes it more believable), and in your case that would be $_____. Typically we get that in the form of a check." And then shut up. You should ask for the check because it saves your company the credit card processing fee (an average of 2 percent). Will you accept a credit card? Of course.

- o Customers may want to negotiate the initial investment amount and put it on a credit card. So...you need to know what the minimal amount is that your company will accept. Remember, without an initial investment, customers may feel that they can cancel the project at any time, and it doesn't matter. But it does matter because your company may have already ordered the materials to make their product. In some states, when you have collected an initial investment, your company will be entitled to keep a portion of that sum, depending on how much has already been spent for materials, processing, and production. Make sure you and your company know what the state laws entitle you to.
- o If the transaction is financed, you still should ask for an initial investment. Why? Because this means the customers have skin in the game, and they are usually reluctant to try to cancel because they believe they could lose their deposit. But, again, remember, if they want to cancel, you should let them. Especially if you are dealing with older customers, whose kids want them to cancel, or if one of the spouses or cosigners dies. The bad word-of-mouth advertising could be lethal for your company. Think about two things: (1) Do you want to be on TV justifying your decision to the local TV troubleshooter? and (2) What's your reputation worth?

- I shouldn't have to say this, but I will because it has happened. *Always* carry a pen (and a spare pen, just in case), so your customers can authorize their paperwork. How embarrassing to ask a customer to get a pen. And never use a pen that is a "clicker." I have seen nervous sales reps click their pens during the presentation, undoubtedly annoying and distracting the customers.

Takeaway Nugget(s) from Element 11:

ELEMENT 12

WARM DOWN

- Time to be memorable, time to laugh, time to shake hands.
- Thank you: It's always a good thing to congratulate your customers on making the decision to do business with you and your company. I've found that another handshake is well received at this time.
- If they did not decide to do business with you, you should still shake hands and say Thank You. To me, a *No* is really a *Maybe*—I translate it to "not at this time, but possibly later." Always leave the door open.
- Repeat how happy they are or will be (if installation or delivery is later).
- Any free things—for example, extended free warranty service calls for participation in a yard-sign program, pen, purse-size hand sanitizer—now is the time to get them out and share. You will be amazed at the positivity you will get from the simplest of gifts. And with your company logo on the gift (this is a *must*), you will become even more memorable.
- Prepare for asking for referrals: Sow the seed for coming back for referrals when you do your follow-up visit. You are *not* entitled to referrals until the project or service is completed and the customers are satisfied.
- Explain your referral program (all great companies have a referral program): Perhaps $100 for every prospect your customers refer to you that purchases and takes delivery of $2,500 or more

of products or services. And you will hand-deliver the check to them. This is an effective way for your customers to earn some extra spending money to use for things like Christmas gifts or a getaway weekend vacation. The $100s can really add up. And maybe you could offer an additional $100 per customer once they have sent you five customers who purchased. Check with your management team first before you begin to make these offers.

- Some companies give customers gift cards (remember, printed with your company logo and a dollar amount only good if used to purchase your products) for customers to give to their family, friends, coworkers, relatives, and neighbors. By the way, if customers ask if they can keep a gift card to use on a subsequent purchase from you, I hope your answer is a speedy and resounding *Yes*!!!!

Takeaway Nugget(s) from Element 12:

ELEMENT 13

WHAT'S NEXT

- Follow-up
  - If you have left a proposal but have not heard back from the customers, it's OK to pick up the phone and call them. An opening line may be as follows: "I was thinking about you and thought I might call to see if you have any additional questions?" *Do not* ask if they have made a purchasing decision yet. If you connected with them during the appointment, they will usually respond to your original question with the answer that you are seeking. You can then ask follow-up questions. If they decided to go with someone else, tell them, "That's OK. They are a fine company, and I am sure they will do a great job for you." Going negative on their decision leaves a bad taste in their mouth and could cause them to tell family, friends, coworkers, relatives, and neighbors about your negativity. Yes, it sucks to lose a sale to your competition, but, as Alfred Lord Tennyson once said, "'tis better to have loved and lost, than never to have loved at all." In other words, take the high road and make this a teaching moment. Ask yourself two questions, and write down the answers: "What did I do well?" and "What could I have done better?"
- Thank You Notes: These should be hand written and mailed to every customer as soon as possible. And by every customer, I mean even those who did not purchase from you. Notes received in the mail have a great impact and sometimes are mentioned

to family, friends, coworker, relatives, and neighbors. E-mails are always deleted, frequently without being read. Do you want to be memorable? If yes, take the time and spend the small amount of money that might bring you future sales.

- After you have made the sale, if there is an installation or a delivery involved, make sure you contact your customers after the installation or delivery to check on everything. If there is an issue, it is best to know it sooner rather than later, so you can make sure it is taken care of. Your customers will be grateful for the call or visit, a nice surprise. This will also be an opportune time to ask for referrals. Caution: Do not promise your customers that you will contact them during the installation or delivery. Things can come up that will prevent you from doing this, and you would disappoint them. Instead, as mentioned above, make it a surprise, and if you can't make it, they will not be disappointed. As a consumer, I always expect the follow-up call or visit, and, yes, it does influence whether or not I will give the company, and sales rep, referrals or good word-of-mouth recommendations. If you are an outstanding sales rep, your goal should be to have at least one-third of your business come from referrals or word-of-mouth recommendations. (Do you know your current referral percentage, and is it greater than one-third?)

- Understand you are entitled to ask for referrals. You have earned them. Also, understand that this is one thing that customers really do not like to do. Oftentimes you will need to work on your "asking for referrals" skills. If you used the Marketing Agreement, and they agreed to provide you with referrals, it's a lot easier. And if they do give you referrals, to make the referrals *great*, ask your customers if they would call the referrals and provide an introduction for you. It costs nothing to ask; you are already at *No*. But what if they said *Yes* and made those calls?

- Call your customers within three months after they receive or begin to use your product or service, just to see how everything is going. If there is an issue, get involved to help them solve it. If everything's OK, this is another good time to ask if they know of anyone who could benefit from what your company has to offer. And you could also ask if there are any other products or services your company offers that they might need. Because your call was unexpected, and they are pleasantly surprised, they may provide a referral or perhaps express an interest in another of your products. These brief follow-up calls always generate additional business for the aggressive sales rep. Think positive when you are making the calls, and results will follow.

- Visiting without notice: If you do decide to visit customers' homes to check on their project or product or service without calling first, leave your car in the drive with the engine running and the car door open. That way, when they answer the door, they will be able to immediately see that you are not planning to stay.
  - If they are not home, write them a note on the back of one of your business cards and leave it on their front door.
  - If you decide to visit a B-to-B client without notice, take only your business card to leave behind. Your lack of a notepad, computer, and so on clearly indicates this is purely a social call.
- The goal of staying in touch with your customers is called TOMA—Top-of-Mind Awareness. So if your customers ever need additional products or services, or their family, friends, coworkers, relatives, or neighbors ever need your products or services for the first time, your name and company will be remembered (and you will have an opportunity for additional sales).
- Want to generate your own appointments?
  - Wear your company's logo wear (and a name badge too!) everywhere you go during your workday (and even weekend days): to breakfast, to stores, to appointments, to the car wash, to lunch, and so on. The more people see your company name, the more they are apt to ask you what you do. This frequently leads to an appointment and subsequent sales. And some companies pay extra for these types of sales since they did not have to spend any advertising dollars to generate it. I think you get the picture—the Big Picture.

Takeaway Nugget(s) from Element 13:

FINAL THOUGHTS

B efore I give you my final thoughts, I wanted to share with you a quick summary of the sales process reduced to four simple steps:

1. Be a friend.
2. Make a friend.
3. Involve your new friend in your product or service.
4. Involve your new friend's friends in your product or service (referral).

OK – HERE ARE MY FINAL THOUGHTS:

Remember, change is a process. It takes time. After finishing this book, buy some lined three-by-five cards and write down on a card three take-away nuggets you want to work on or change. Carry this card around with you at all times, and when one of the nuggets you have written down becomes part of your sales process, draw a line through it. After you have drawn a line through two of the three items, take another card and transfer the one nugget that still needs to be done to the new card. Then add two more nuggets. Start the process over. Take the used card with the lined-out nuggets and put it in a drawer. After three months, review the stack of cards in the drawer and see how much progress you have made. I am sure you will be amazed at the number of changes you have made, as well as how much your paycheck reflects the positive changes.

Quoting a line from the movie *The Natural*: "I believe we have two lives. The life we learn with, and the life we live with after we learn."

And so I have to ask you:

"What will you do with your sales life now that you have learned?"

About the Author

R ik Vonderhaar is a sales and marketing expert with more than forty-one years of experience delivering results to Fortune 500 companies and small businesses. His specialties include home improvement and financial services. Now retired, Vonderhaar shares his wealth of knowledge and proven techniques as a volunteer consultant with the nonprofit business community in Cincinnati, Ohio, where he was born and resides with his wife, Sandy, to whom he has been married for over forty-one years. His greatest accomplishments are his two children and three grandsons.

Made in the USA
Columbia, SC
12 September 2018